The American Revolution

Contents

oming to America On a pleasant summer day in 1750, a ship carrying 400 Germans arrived at the docks in Philadelphia. These newcomers were about to begin new lives in America.

Now if this had been a hundred years earlier, the arrival of 400 **immigrants** would have been big news. Back then, 400 new immigrants would have been a big addition to any colony. In fact, back then there were only five English colonies in North America. Some colonies didn't "struggle." Colonists struggled just to keep their tiny settlements going.

Not in 1750, though. By this time there were 13 colonies, and all of them were strong and growing. Almost every week a ship arrived with another boatload of new Americans. The population of the colonies had already passed 1 million, and was fast climbing toward 2 million. Settlements had spread from the Atlantic Ocean as far west as the Appalachian Mountains.

Why had so many people come to the British colonies in America? Why were so many still coming in 1750? The answer lies in one word: opportunity. Opportunity to own land of their own. Opportunity to work in America's growing towns and cities. Opportunity to worship as they pleased. Opportunity to start a new life.

And who were these colonists, these new Americans? Where were they from? They were ordinary people, mainly—farmers and people from small towns. Most were from England. But a large number—perhaps a third of them—came from other countries. One of the largest groups was Germans.

> **vocabulary**
> **immigrant** a person from one country who comes into another country to live there

Another large group was the Scots-Irish, who were Scottish people living in the northern part of Ireland. There were Swedes and Finns, Scots and Welsh, Dutch and Swiss, French and Irish.

Not all Americans of 1750 had come to the colonies willingly. About one in every five Americans were slaves who were dragged here from Africa. Most lived in the South, but there were slaves in the North, too. Only a small number of blacks were free. Even freedom, though, did not lead to much opportunity for black people in colonial America.

More than nine out of ten colonial families lived on farms. They farmed their land by themselves. With each member of the family pitching in, they produced nearly everything they needed, plus a little bit more for sale. They raised their own food. They cut and sewed their own clothes from animal hides and wool. They made their own furniture. Most of them even built the houses they lived in.

There were still only four or five cities in all of the colonies, and just a handful of towns. But the cities were growing quickly. In just a few more years, Philadelphia would become the second largest city in the whole British Empire. (London, England, was the largest.)

What sparked this growth of towns and cities? Trade, mainly trade with other countries. From the docks of the cities on the coast, merchants sent lumber, fur, salted fish, flour, and tobacco to many parts of the world. To those docks, ships returned with glass, paint, tea, wine, and other goods the colonists wanted.

Trade meant jobs. Men loaded and unloaded ships. They built boats. They made sails, rope, and barrels for shipping goods. But cities and towns offered other kinds of work also. Men, and some women, ran stores and shops. Skilled workers baked bread and made pots and pans. They printed newspapers. They made fine shoes and clothes for other city dwellers.

As you see, Americans were a busy, hardworking people. They believed that hard work would pay off in a better life. Except for the slaves, it did. It is true that compared to Europe there were few really rich people in America. But there were few really poor people either. It was a good land to live in.

A log cabin could make a snug home for a frontier family.

Staying Apart and Coming Together

When people arrived in the American colonies, they tried to settle near others from the same homeland. This made them feel more comfortable in a strange, new land. They could speak their own language and follow their own ways of life. They wore the same kind of clothing they had worn in their homeland and built the same kind of houses.

In time, however, something interesting and important happened. Immigrant groups began to borrow ideas and customs from each other. For example, consider the log cabin. Swedes had built log cabins in their homeland. Here in America, they found plenty of trees for doing the same. A log cabin was easy to put up. Two strong men with axes could build one in a couple of weeks. Other groups came to America with their own ideas of how a house should look. But then they saw these log cabins. They realized that these buildings were perfect for life on the **frontier.** Soon it made no difference what group the frontier settlers were part of. They all built log cabins.

All this borrowing among immigrant groups even changed

> **vocabulary**
> **frontier** the newly settled area on the edge of the unsettled area or wilderness

3

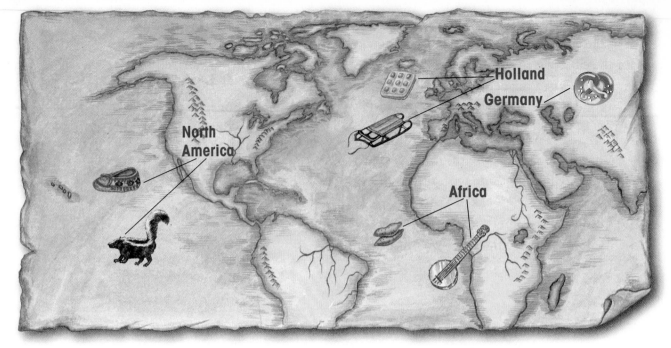

English, as it is spoken in the United States, has borrowed words from many cultures.

the way Americans talked. Most colonists spoke English, but English began to borrow words from the other languages in the colonies. From German came *noodle, pretzel,* and *kindergarten.* From Dutch came *waffle, cookie,* and *sleigh. Pecan, moccasin, skunk,* and *squash* came from Native American languages. And African languages contributed lots of words, including *yams, banjo,* and *tote.*

The result of all this borrowing became a new kind of English—American English. And little by little, this new American English became the language of the children and grandchildren of immigrants from other lands. Borrowings like these helped to bring the different groups of colonists closer together.

Better Roads

By the 1750s, the colonists were also being brought together by improved roads. You would not think of these roads as very good compared to our own. They were narrow, often muddy, and filled with tree stumps. Still, they were better than the roads of 50 or 100 years earlier. These roads made it possible for more Americans to travel and led to increased trade among the colonies.

Better roads also improved communications, by speeding up the exchange of information. By the 1750s, mail was being delivered between Philadelphia and Boston in just three days. That meant that newspapers printed in the cities could be quickly delivered to colonists in the countryside. Everyone in a colony could read the same news and stay informed about the same things. In all these ways, then, colonists of many different backgrounds were starting to come together. They were beginning—just beginning, of course—to have more things in common.

As you will see, that soon became very important in what was about to happen in the American colonies.

rowing Up What would it have been like to grow up in colonial America? Let's spend a little time finding out. We'll begin with your family. It's probably a farm family. Nine out of ten colonial families are.

Chances are that your house is pretty crowded. That's because colonists have large families. Nearly all women marry, and most have seven or eight children.

There might be another reason your house is so crowded, though. You see, in the world of the 1700s, lots of people die young. It's not unusual for a parent to die. When that happens, the remaining parent usually remarries—often to another person who also has many children. So you're pretty sure to have lots of brothers and sisters. And there's a good chance you have some stepbrothers and stepsisters, too.

With a crowd like that, what do you think are the chances that you have your own bedroom? Just about zero. You not only don't have your own bedroom; you don't even have your own bed. You share a bed with two or three other children in the family, and you hope they all sleep without kicking about.

Actually, you're probably grateful to have so many kids in the family because they are your "built-in" playmates. You don't have neighborhood friends, because you don't have a neighborhood. Only people in the villages and towns have neighborhoods. Farmhouses are far apart. So the children in the family depend on each other for lots of things, including play.

Of course everyone has regular chores to do. That includes you. Everyone's day begins at dawn, if not before.

Nature provided a playground for colonial farm children.

If you are a boy, your first job is to bring in firewood and build the fire. Matches don't exist yet, so you hope there is still a burning coal in the fireplace from the night before. If not, you'll have to start a new fire or run to the next farmhouse in the cold morning air, carrying a metal box or tongs for bringing back a "live" coal.

After breakfast and morning prayers, it's out to the fields with your father. You'll plant and hoe and clear away brush from new land that's to be planted next year. Maybe you'll help repair a fence or two.

If you are a girl, you'll be helping your mother make candles and preserve foods, starting right after breakfast. You'll probably also have to feed the animals. Then you'll spend the rest of the morning helping to cook the noon meal. That's the main meal of the day. In the afternoon you'll sew, knit, weave, or spin yarn.

Did you notice there was no time in your day's schedule for school? That's because you probably don't go to school. Perhaps you did last year and the year before. But you can

Slave children had to grow up quickly and work like adults.

read and write now. Most parents feel that once you can do that, you don't need any more school.

In fact, you may not have gone to school at all. Chances are that you learned to read and write at home. An older brother or sister or maybe a parent started teaching you when you were five or six. If no one in your home could read, then you might have been sent to learn at another farmhouse where someone could.

It's amazing, though. Even though only a small number of colonial children went to school, nearly all of them learned to read. Parents believed it was important. Children were told it was important. And that was that. They learned.

Children of Slaves

If you were a child in a slave family on a southern plantation, your life would be very different. When you were much younger—say five or six—there had been plenty of time for play. In fact, some of your playmates were probably the children of your owner. You fished and picked berries with them, and you and they wandered over the plantation to-gether, moving about freely.

Then, when you reached seven or eight years old, you started to take care of younger brothers and sisters. Also, your owner began to give you some regular tasks, like sweeping the yard and feeding the chickens, the same kinds of jobs that free white children did on family farms. Even at that age, however, you were already starting to understand that you were not the same as those free white children. Your parents taught you to be careful how you talked to members of the owner's family. You began to see some grown-ups, maybe even members of your own family, being badly treated or even whipped.

The big change in your life, though, is coming just as you reach your present age. Now is when you begin life as a grown-up slave. You work in the fields, doing the same hard work as adults. You plant, you plow, and you pick cotton, from sunup to sundown. You can be punished for not working hard enough or for not showing enough politeness to the master's family or for anything at all.

Even if your parents know that reading is important, you will probably never learn to read. The laws actually forbid anyone to teach you to read. Reading, you see, is dangerous to the slave system. You might get "dangerous" ideas about freedom from reading.

Sickness and Cures

Sickness is a serious problem in every colonial home. Many children die from disease before they reach your age. Little is really known about why people get sick or how they can get well and stay well.

A lot of people think they know, though. They make their own medicines

Herbs were an important source of medicine for the colonists.

from plants called herbs and also from the roots and bark of trees. Do you have a cut that isn't healing? A swelling that won't go down? A bad cold, perhaps? There's sure to be an herb or a root that will cure you.

Actually, some of these herbs have been used for hundreds of years and really do seem to do some good. Others, though—well . . .

There are also some special tricks that are supposed to help you get better. For example, to bring down a fever, your parents might cut your toenails and put them into a small linen bag. Then they would tie the bag around the neck of an eel and put the eel in a tub of water. When the eel died, your fever was supposed to go down. One of the best-educated men in the Massachusetts colony has recommended that cure.

Even if you are just feeling tired and need pepping up, there's a special recipe to help. You roast a toad, grind it up, and add boiling water to make a kind of tea. Drink it and

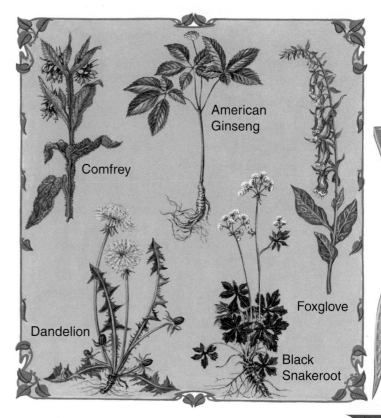

Comfrey

American Ginseng

Dandelion

Foxglove

Black Snakeroot

Colonial doctors often relied on remedies we wouldn't recognize today.

1. Feed your children only plain foods and not much sugar, spice, or salt. No eating between meals, except for dry bread.

2. Keep them away from candy.

3. See that they sleep on a hard bed. No soft feathers.

4. Bathe them in cold water, even in the winter.

5. Give them very thin shoes that will leak and let in water. (A famous man got this idea by noting that poor people often went bare-foot and didn't seem to get sick from that.)

6. Strawberries, cherries, and gooseberries are good for children. Melons, peaches, plums, and grapes are not, even though they are tasty. Don't give them any.

you'll be feeling lively in no time. For a cold or a sore throat, sprinkle pepper on a piece of meat and wrap it around your throat.

Of course, you could go to a doctor. There are a few doctors in the colonies. But it probably won't do much good. There are no special schools for training doctors in the colonies, so doctors don't know much more than most others about making people well. Doctors do have a favorite cure for almost any illness, though. They cut open a vein in your arm and let about a cup of blood run out before stopping the wound. This is called "bleeding the patient."

Of course the best thing to do is to stay well. Your parents have been told to do quite a few things to keep you from getting sick. See the list above for a few of them.

Many of our great American leaders grew up following rules like these. But our history books don't tell us whether they enjoyed it! As you see, growing up in colonial times was quite different from what it is today. Based on what you've read so far, do you think you might have liked it?

Part of the Empire If bumper stickers had existed in colonial days, one of them surely would have said, "Proud to Be British." For that's how American colonists felt in the middle of the 1700s.

The English Parliament has two houses, the House of Lords and the House of Commons. This is a House of Commons meeting during the eighteenth century.

British navy, the greatest navy in the world. Most important, as members of the British Empire, American colonists enjoyed a great deal of self-government. That is, colonists had a say in choosing their own leaders and making their own laws. Here's how that came about. Self-government started in England several hundred years earlier. At that time, certain wealthy and important English landowners elected people to represent them in the English Parliament. Parliament is a law-making body, much like our Congress.

They were members of the greatest empire in the world—the British Empire, which had colonies all over the world. They could trade with any part of the empire, while other peoples, for the most part, could not. On the oceans, their ships were protected by the

At first, Parliament didn't have much power. The king had most of it. But over time, members of Parliament insisted that only they, not the king, should make decisions where taxes and spending were concerned. They said that Parliament should have a say in making other laws, too.

English kings did not agree. For a couple of hundred years, Parliament and the king struggled over this issue. Parliament finally won.

When the English began to settle in America, they brought along their ideas of self-government. Pretty soon, colonists were voting for representatives to their own law-making bodies. These were usually called **assemblies.** That doesn't mean that everyone in the colonies could vote. Women could not. Blacks could not. Native Americans could not. Only white males who owned land or other property could vote. But most white males did own land, so a large part of the colonial population could vote.

> **vocabulary**
> **assembly** a group of representatives who gather to make laws

Soon colonists were insisting that only their elected assemblies could make laws for their colonies. Of course, they knew that it was Parliament's job to run the whole British Empire. It was up to Parliament to pass laws about trade between different parts of the empire. Only Parliament could decide the rules for trade between the empire and other parts of the world. The American colonists didn't argue about that.

When it came to everyday life in their own colony, though, what could a Parliament 3,000 miles away know about such things? Only their own elected representatives could understand what kinds of laws were needed and what kinds were foolish. Therefore, they said, only its own elected assembly could make laws for a colony.

That was especially true about tax laws. You'll want to remember that point, because it's going to become very important. As the colonists saw it, *they could be taxed only by their own elected representatives.* Anything else would be "taxation without representation." Englishmen had long ago fought and won the battle against that.

Americans Claim British Rights

The people of Great Britain—the English, but also the Scots and the Welsh—enjoyed other rights and liberties, too. As members of the British Empire, American colonists felt they had these same rights.

Most of these rights and liberties were meant to protect the people against unfair actions by their own government. Here's one example: The government could not just take away a person's house or land or ship or other property. If the government said it really needed that property for some very important purpose, it would have to prove that to a judge. Even if the judge agreed with the government, the government still had to pay the owner for it.

Here's another: Government officers could not just show up and search your home or business whenever they felt like it. They first had to explain to a judge why they believed you were hiding something illegal. The judge then had to give permission for the officers to conduct a search. Otherwise, no search was allowed.

Here are two more important rights that English people had. They could not be put in jail unless they were accused of breaking a law. And if they were accused, they couldn't just be kept in jail indefinitely. They had the right to a trial before a jury of fellow citizens. A jury is a group of people who hear the facts of the case and then decide whether the person is guilty or innocent. Also, no secret accusations or secret evidence are permitted. Everything has to be out in the open, so that accused persons can defend themselves.

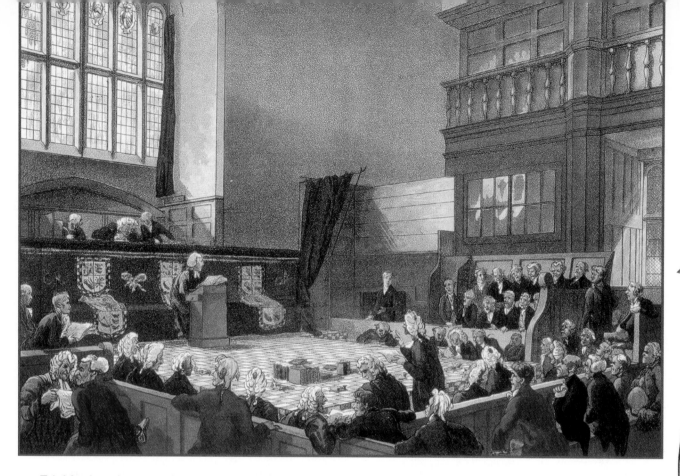

Trial by jury is a very important right, both in English courts, shown here, and American courts. In this picture, the judge sits under the windows on the left and the jury sits under the windows on the right.

There were other rights, too. If citizens wanted to get together peaceably to talk about a problem or to protest something, the government could not interfere. And if they wanted to petition their government—that is, to ask the government to change a law or do something, or stop doing something— well, they had that right, too.

Do these rights seem very special to you? Maybe not. That's because we have them today, and we tend to take them for granted. But the sad truth is that, even today, most people in the world do not enjoy these rights. In the middle of the 1700s, very few people outside the British Empire did. British people were proud to have "the rights of Englishmen," and so were the American colonists.

No wonder American colonists felt they were among the most fortunate people on earth. They lived in a land blessed by nature. They enjoyed rights and liberties equal to anyone, anywhere in the world. They were proud and happy to be a part of the empire of Great Britain. Probably the idea of separating from Great Britain never entered a colonist's head. Thinking back to that time, Benjamin Franklin many years later recalled, "I never heard in any conversation from any person . . . the least [desire] for separation from England."

Ben Franklin was remembering how the colonists felt around 1763. But 13 years later the American colonies separated from England and declared their independence. You are about to learn what happened to make the colonists change their minds.

Whose Land Is It? Traveling 500 miles through the wilderness was a long way to go to deliver a message. That's 500 miles there and 500 miles back. It must have seemed especially long to the 21-year-old military officer from Virginia who delivered the messages because all he got for his troubles was a big No.

The young officer and his party of six were from the British colony of Virginia. They were members of the Virginia **militia,** a sort of volunteer citizen's army. At that time—the year was 1753—France had built a string of forts along the Ohio River, in what is now western Pennsylvania. The young officer's mission was to carry a message from the governor of Virginia to the French general in charge of those forts.

> **vocabulary**
> **militia** a body of armed citizens prepared for military service at any time

For weeks the Virginians traveled by horseback and canoe until they finally met up with the French general. The young officer handed him the message. This is what it said: Your forts are on Virginia's land. Get out!

The French general was polite but firm. No, he replied, my troops will not get out. This land belongs to France. French fur trappers have lived on this land for a hundred years. French colonists have started settlements here. The forts will stay right where they are.

On the return journey the group's horses gave out, and the officer and his men had to walk much of the way. Along the way an Indian fired at the officer, just barely missing him. Then, while crossing an ice-filled river on a raft, the officer was accidentally knocked overboard. He nearly drowned before his men finally fished him out.

The men finally returned to Virginia, and the officer gave the governor the bad news. The French were determined to stay.

The young officer's unsuccessful journey would soon lead to war. That war in turn led to events that brought about the birth of the United States of America.

And the 21-year-old officer from the Virginia colony? He would have a lot to do with the birth of the United States of America, too. His name was George Washington.

Washington's Mistakes

The governor of the Virginia colony was determined to make the French leave the land near the Ohio River. The next year, 1754, he sent George Washington to the west again. This time Washington led a force of 150 men.

The British had built a small fort at the point where two rivers come together to form the Ohio River. Washington was to join forces with the British soldiers at the fort. However, before he got there, Washington learned that the French had already captured the fort and renamed it Fort Duquesne (doo KAYN).

George Washington, on the white horse, was proud to be an officer in the Virginia militia.

In time, George Washington would become a great general. But just then, he was young and inexperienced. He proceeded to make a number of mistakes. Since Washington did not have enough men to drive the French out of the fort, the wisest thing to do would have been to return to Virginia. Instead, he continued on with his small force.

Along the way his troops surprised and defeated a group of 30 French soldiers, killing ten of them. The French at Fort Duquesne had many more men than Washington did, and they had Indian **allies** as well. They were now sure to send out a larger force from the fort to deal with Washington's Virginians.

When he realized this, Washington built a makeshift camp his men called Fort Necessity. The spot Washington chose for Fort Necessity was a low piece of ground. Soon after the French attacked Fort Necessity, it began to rain heavily. Before long, Washington's men, their guns, and their gunpowder were soaked with the rain that collected in their low area. The Virginians fought bravely, but after nine hours, Washington had to surrender.

The French commander then instructed an assistant to prepare a statement about why the fighting had taken place. We, the Virginians, said the statement, are the ones who started the fighting. It was all our fault. The French commander read the statement and then handed it to Washington. "Sign," he said. "Sign, or I will not allow the prisoners to return to Virginia." Washington signed, and the men were released.

> **vocabulary**
> **ally** a nation that has promised to help another nation in wartime

When the men returned to Virginia, British officials were very angry—not just at the French but at Washington. They blamed him for his unwise decisions. They also blamed him for signing the statement. Washington resigned from the Virginia militia. That could have been the end of his military career. If it had been, perhaps we would all be saluting the British flag today instead of the Stars and Stripes.

The French and Indian War

War in the Colonies Washington's small battle against the French was the start of the French and Indian War. On one side were France, the French colonists in America, and their Indian allies. On the other side were Great Britain, the British colonists in America, and their Indian allies.

Great Britain and France had been fighting each other on and off for nearly a hundred years. No one was surprised that they were doing it again. Each of these European countries had colonies in other parts of the world. Each wanted to grab the other's colonies. So it was also no surprise when the war that began in the woods of North America was soon being fought on two other continents and on the Atlantic, Pacific, and Indian oceans as well. In Europe and Asia the war came to be called the Seven Years' War.

Fighting in the Woods

The British were determined to take Fort Duquesne and drive the French out of the Ohio River valley. In 1755 they sent General Edward Braddock with 2,200 troops from their regular full-time army to do the job. Eager to join Braddock's army and return to Fort Duquesne, George Washington wrote the British general and offered his services. Braddock appointed the eager young Virginian a colonel (KER null), in charge of 450 colonial soldiers.

Braddock was an experienced general. He knew a lot about fighting wars in Europe, where armies battled on great open fields. But he knew nothing about fighting a war in the woods of North America. Worse, he was too stubborn to listen to anyone who did.

The first thing Braddock did was order his men to cut a hundred-mile-long road through the woods toward Fort Duquesne so that his army could march over it—almost as if they were on parade.

Colonel Washington knew that was unwise. He and his colonists knew something about the woods. They warned Braddock that his troops should advance with great caution. They warned that an attack could come at any time and from any quarter. But Braddock ignored their advice. After all, they were mere colonists. What did they know about the art of war? A few miles from Fort Duquesne, French soldiers and their Indian allies attacked Braddock's army suddenly and without warning. They fired from hiding places in the thick woods. The British didn't know what had hit them. Their bright red coats made them easy targets. They panicked and ran, and General Braddock was killed.

It was fortunate for the British that George Washington had gone along. Courageously exposing himself to danger, Washington managed to lead what was left of the British army to safety. During the fighting, Washington had two horses shot from under him. He later also found that four bullets had passed through his clothing. A few more inches one way or the other, and the history of our country might have turned out differently.

Victory for the British

For a time the war went badly for the British elsewhere, too. Then William Pitt took charge of Great Britain's foreign affairs. This included foreign wars and dealing with the colonies.

It was true that the war was being fought in several different parts of the world and that North America was only one of them. But Pitt knew how valuable the American colonies were to Great Britain. He was determined that Great Britain must win this war and keep control of its North American lands. If it took more troops, Pitt would send them. If it took more ships, Pitt would get those, too. All this cost a lot of money, but Pitt was ready to spend whatever was necessary to win.

Pitt also saw that the key to victory in North America was to win control of two rivers—the St. Lawrence River and the Niagara River. These were the rivers the French used to send supplies to their troops near the Great Lakes and in the Ohio River valley, including those at Fort Duquesne. If the British could prevent the French from using these rivers—well, you can see what would happen to the French armies. They would soon run out of supplies. And without supplies, all their bravery and fighting skills would do them no good.

That's why Pitt sent these instructions to the British armies in America: Get control of the St. Lawrence and the Niagara rivers, no matter what it takes. Aided by their Indian allies and by the American colonists, the British did just that. In addition, British and American troops captured Fort Duquesne. They renamed it Fort Pitt, which is how the city of Pittsburgh got its name.

The dying General Braddock was carried from the battlefield.

Painting: Braddock's Retreat, July 9th 1755; (n.p.); 1865, Creator—Alonzo Chappel. Courtesy, Chicago Historical Society.

A great British victory at the Battle of Quebec in Canada finished off the French. The city of Quebec sits atop steep cliffs alongside the St. Lawrence River. The cliffs secured the city from attack—or so it was thought until one night in 1759. That night, British troops led by General James Wolfe climbed those cliffs and reached the top. When dawn broke, the French found the British assembled on a flat area at the top called the Plains of Abraham, ready to do battle. The British defeated the French troops and took the city of Quebec. Both Wolfe and the French general, Louis Montcalm, lost their lives in this famous battle.

The British now controlled the St. Lawrence River, and the French knew they had lost. In 1763, Great Britain and France made peace. In the peace treaty, France gave all of Canada to Great Britain. France also gave up all the land between the Appalachian Mountains and the Mississippi River to Great Britain. The land west of the Mississippi River was given to Spain, one of France's partners in the war.

How complete was Great Britain's victory? This is how complete: Before the war, France claimed four or five times as much land in North America as did Great Britain. After the war, France had next to none. Britain was now the main European colonial power in North America.

Notice how much territory France lost in North America as a result of the French and Indian War.

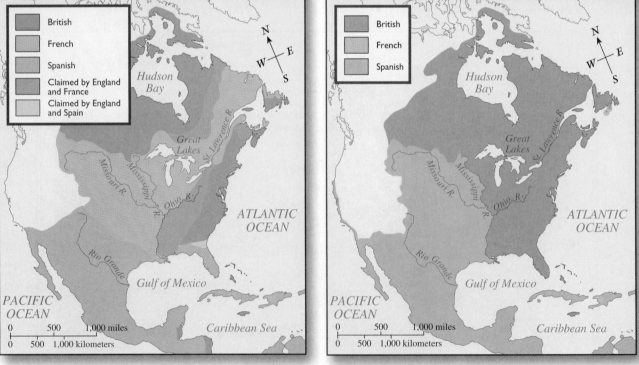

Colonists Claim New Land What's the point of winning a lot of land in a war if you're not allowed to use it? Even before the French and Indian War, some colonists had moved onto the land between the Appalachian Mountains and the Mississippi River.

Now that France had given up any claim to this land, many more colonists looked forward to having it all for themselves. To the British government, however, the matter looked rather different. True, France was gone from this land. But the area was hardly empty. It was the homeland of many groups of Native Americans. Some of them had been allies of the British and fought in the war against the French.

Those Indians did not want white settlers taking their lands. Some Indian tribes had united behind a chief of the Ottawa tribe named Pontiac to drive out white settlers who were already there and to keep any more from coming. Indian warriors captured British forts and killed hundreds of settlers before British troops were finally able to end the uprising.

Now that they had finished one war with France, the British did not want a new one with the Indians. They would surely have one, though, if their American colonists kept pushing onto Indian lands.

Great Britain believed that, for the time being at least, it would be best to keep the settlers out of the Indians' homelands. On a map of North America, the new British king, George III, drew a line running along the top of the Appalachian Mountains from New York all the way south to Georgia. Then he issued a proclamation: until further notice,

Native Americans attacked forts like this one to keep settlers out of their homeland.

no more colonists were allowed to settle west of that line.

This Proclamation of 1763 angered the colonists. They had not fought the French to win this land for the Indians. They expected to get it for themselves. Now their own king was telling them they couldn't move there. Not only that, the king also announced that thousands of British troops would be stationed along the frontier to keep peace between the colonists and the Indians. To the colonists that meant stopping them from building houses and farms west of George III's line.

The Quarrel Grows

Soon the colonies had an even bigger quarrel with Great Britain. Like the quarrel over the Proclamation of 1763, this one grew out of the war with France.

To win that war, Britain had poured money into ships and men and supplies—more money than the British government had. So the government borrowed what it needed. Now it had to pay this money back. Also, the government would need money to pay for the troops who were to be stationed in forts on the American frontier.

Where was all this money to come from? To Parliament, the answer was clear. From the colonists of course. Not all of it, maybe, but certainly their fair share. The colonists gained a great benefit from Britain's victory over France, didn't they? Let them help pay for it.

First, said Parliament, let's make the colonists start paying the taxes they *should* have been paying all along but haven't. For example, colonists were supposed to pay taxes on certain goods brought in from elsewhere, or imported. Instead, they had been smuggling—bringing in the goods secretly—to avoid the eyes of the tax collectors.

So the British government sent more officials to America to make sure the colonists paid the taxes, especially those on sugar and molasses. Even worse, these officials were allowed to enter and search colonists' homes and businesses *without the owner's permission*. They could search for smuggled goods or for any other evidence to show that colonists had broken the law.

Trees were the most available building material for frontier forts.

Do you remember the "rights of Englishmen?" Didn't one of those rights say that government officials could not just show up and search your home or business whenever they felt like it? How could their own British government take away this right from the colonists? Parliament came up with still another way to squeeze money from the colonies. When the French and Indian War ended, there were thousands of British troops in the colonies. The British government wanted to keep them there. So to help pay for them, Parliament passed the Quartering Act. This law required the colonial governments to furnish quarters—that is, places to live—for all these troops.

Americans had a big problem with that. Why does the British government want to keep troops in our colonies, they asked? For our protection? Protection against whom? Could it be that there is another reason for keeping troops here—like, to make us obey British laws we think are unfair? And on top of that, they expect us to pay for these troops?

Tax on Paper There was still another way to collect money from the colonists: new taxes. In 1765, Parliament passed the Stamp Act. This law made the colonists pay a tax on just about every imaginable kind of printed paper—about 50 items in all.

Under this law you would have to buy special tax stamps from a tax collector. Then you would stick one on each of the taxed items you used. So every time you bought a newspaper, you'd pay a tax. Every time you bought a copy of your minister's sermon, you'd pay a tax. Every time you bought a calendar, a marriage license, or any kind of legal or business paper, you'd pay a tax. You'd even be taxed on playing cards.

The colonists had been upset by the Proclamation of 1763. They had been angered by the officials searching their homes and businesses. Now they were outraged! No way, said the colonists, are we going to pay that tax on paper. No way.

Do you see why the colonists were so outraged? Was it their own colonial assemblies that had passed this tax law? No, it wasn't. It was the British Parliament in faraway London, England. Colonists did not elect the members of Parliament. Colonists were not represented in Parliament. Then what right did Parliament have to pass a law taxing them? None. Absolutely none. This was "taxation without representation," said the colonists. Here was the British government trampling on yet another right the colonists believed was theirs.

One colonist who strongly protested the Stamp Act was a 29-year-old Virginian named Patrick Henry. Patrick Henry was a member of the Virginia assembly, known as the Virginia House of Burgesses. He made a fiery speech denouncing this new tax. He warned that the Stamp Act would take away the colonists' liberty. Henry's speech was printed in newspapers throughout the colonies. The speech gave people a lot to think about.

Colonists did more than just talk and complain about the Stamp Act. In New York, Boston, Newport, and other places throughout the colonies, they formed groups called the Sons of Liberty. These groups threatened the stamp tax collectors. They even beat up some

Stamps such as this one attached to a document showed that a tax had been paid, in this case five shillings.

of them. Many a stamp tax collector decided that the wisest thing to do was get out of town and just forget about selling the tax stamps.

That wasn't all the Sons of Liberty did. They organized a **boycott** of British goods. That is, they got people to agree not to buy goods from Great Britain. And they said they would not buy them again while the Stamp Act was law.

There were Daughters of Liberty, too. These women helped make the boycott work by making homemade cloth. That way the colonists could get the cloth they needed without buying it from British merchants.

Sons of Liberty, Daughters of Liberty, and the many other people who supported the colonists' cause gave themselves another name. They called themselves Patriots.

The actions didn't stop there. Some leaders called for a special meeting of all the colonies to decide what else to do. Nine colonies sent delegates, or representatives, to the meeting, which was held in New York. The delegates agreed on a number of statements about the rights of colonists. They also asked Parliament to **repeal** the hated law. This meeting of delegates came to be called the Stamp Act Congress.

All these actions by the colonists shocked the leaders of the British government. They were especially worried by the meeting of the Stamp Act Congress. Never before had the American colonies acted together against the British government. British leaders did not want this to become a habit. British merchants weren't

happy either. The boycott was causing them to lose a lot of money.

In 1766, after only one year, Parliament did repeal the Stamp Act. When the news reached America, colonists lit great bonfires in celebration. Through their resistance they had brought an end to the hated Stamp Act. Of course they still loved their king. And no one was talking about leaving the British Empire. It had all been just a family quarrel. Hadn't it?

Bostonians protested the Stamp Act by burning the tax stamps.

ho Is in Charge? You might think Parliament would get the message: No taxation without representation. The colonists had drawn the line there. But the British government still needed money. And now it also needed to show the colonists who was boss.

So in 1767—just one year after repealing the Stamp Act—Parliament tried again. This time it placed taxes on glass, paint, tea, lead, paper, and a number of other goods that colonists imported. This was Parliament's thinking: The colonists need these goods, so when ships deliver them to colonial harbors, our officials will be there to collect the tax. Parliament made things worse by saying that whoever was arrested for not paying the tax would be tried *without a jury.*

Clearly, Parliament didn't understand how determined the colonists were. Once again, taxation without representation? And trial without a jury? So much for the "rights of Englishmen!"

Once again the Sons of Liberty swung into action. They organized another boycott of all British goods. This boycott was as successful as the first one. Meanwhile, the colonists began to make their own paint, lead, glass, and paper. Maybe the quality wasn't as good as what they used to get from Great Britain. And maybe it cost a little more to make. But it would do. It would do.

The new boycott lasted for nearly three years. Once again the Americans succeeded. British merchants and manufacturers were losing so much money because of the boycott that they demanded that Parliament repeal the new taxes.

It was one thing for the colonists to demand that Parliament repeal a tax. Parliament could ignore them if it wished. But Parliament could hardly ignore the powerful businessmen of their own country.

So in 1770, Parliament did repeal the new taxes—all but one of them. They kept the tax on tea. In reply the colonists ended their boycott of all goods from England—all but one of them. You can guess which one. Tea.

Parliament had left the tax on tea to show that it *had* the right to tax the colonists. And the colonists left the boycott on tea to show that Parliament *did not have* the right to tax them. Each side was willing to leave it at that for the time being. By the way, the colonists, who were big tea drinkers, didn't really do without tea. They simply bought it from Dutch merchants who smuggled it into the colonies.

Colonists showed their dislike of the Stamp Act in many ways.

British troops drill on Boston Common.

The Boston Massacre

Meanwhile, more British troops arrived to join those already in the colonies. Colonists were suspicious. The British said the soldiers were needed to defend the colonists against Indian attacks. If that were really so, asked the colonists, then why weren't they on the frontier, where the Indians were? Why were so many in eastern cities, like Philadelphia, New York, and Boston? The troops seemed to be everywhere—on the street corners, in front of buildings, in the parks.

Colonists were angered by the sight of soldiers on their streets day and night. "What can be worse to a people who have tasted the sweets of liberty!" wrote an important Boston minister. As long as the troops remain, he continued, "there will never be harmony between Great Britain and her colonies." And what if a fight should break out between the citizens and the troops? In that case, said this minister, "the moment any blood is shed, all affection will cease." In other words, any good feelings that remained between the colonists and their mother country would end.

The citizens of Boston jeered at the soldiers. They made fun of them. They tried to make their lives miserable. In several cities, fights broke out between colonists and soldiers.

Those fights were not nearly as bad, though, as what happened in Boston on the evening of March 5, 1770. There, a crowd of men and boys gathered around a lone British soldier on guard duty. They shouted insults at him. They threw snowballs at him, some with rocks inside them.

The frightened soldier called for help. More British soldiers arrived. The crowd grew larger. The shouts, the dares, and the insults grew louder and angrier.

Suddenly someone—to this day, no one knows who—called out "Fire!" The soldiers turned their guns on the rioting crowd and shot. When the smoke cleared, five colonists lay dead or wounded, their blood staining the snow-covered street. One of them was Crispus Attucks, a runaway slave who worked as a sailor. Crispus Attucks was the first black American to die for the cause of American liberty, but not the last.

A few days later, more than half the population of Boston turned out for a funeral march for the dead men. Shops were closed. Church bells rang. Angry Bostonians called the killing a *massacre*—a needless killing of defenseless people. The event became known as the Boston Massacre.

A Boston silversmith named Paul Revere made a copper engraving that showed soldiers firing on a group of perfectly peaceful, innocent citizens. You can print many paper copies from a single engraving, and Revere did.

No one knows for sure whether he really saw the shooting. And some of the things shown in the engraving are not true. But Paul Revere was a Son of Liberty. The reason he made that engraving was that he wanted to make people angry at the British. Never mind that the citizens who were shot had been asking for trouble all night. They certainly did not deserve to die for that.

So that is what comes of having all these troops around, said the colonists. Where will this all end?

The colonists and the British reacted differently to this picture by Paul Revere. Can you tell why?

Calm Before the Storm In time, the anger following the Boston Massacre died down, as anger often does. The British government didn't do any new things to upset the American colonists. The American colonists didn't do any new things to upset the British government. The next three years were mostly a period of calm.

But important changes were starting to occur in the way many colonists thought about England. Countries that set up colonies in other lands are often called "mother countries." That's what most colonists had always called England. Even those who had never set foot in England called that country "home."

The British used the same words to describe their relationship with the colonies. Even William Pitt, who was a great friend of the American colonies, said, "This is the mother country, they are the children. They must obey, and we prescribe [give the orders]."

But children grow up. They develop their own abilities. They discover they can do many things for themselves. They gain confidence. They feel they need to do things their own way. And eventually, they leave home to live their own lives. Independently.

In the years after the Boston Massacre, some American colonists wondered out loud whether that time had now arrived for them. This change in thinking came slowly. At first only a few felt that way. And even most of those people still wanted to remain in the British Empire. They were still loyal to their king. They just thought it was time for Parliament and the whole British government to stop making rules for them.

A small number of colonists, though, talked about going much further. They believed that Americans could only keep their liberties by breaking away from the British Empire completely. The colonies, they said, must become independent.

Sam Adams

Sam Adams of Boston felt that way. Adams came from an important Boston family. He lost most of his family's money because he was not very good at business. Maybe it's more correct to say that he just wasn't very interested in business. He had other things on his mind. Back in 1765, at the time of the Stamp Act, Sam Adams had organized the Sons of Liberty. He had been a leader in the boycott against British goods during the Stamp Act crisis. He

This portrait of Sam Adams shows him with documents that symbolize his work with the Committees of Correspondence.

had led another boycott when the British government tried to tax goods the colonies imported.

Ever since that time, Adams had been trying to convince colonists that the time had arrived to separate from Great Britain. In newspaper articles he urged his fellow colonists to stand up against Britain for their rights. "The liberties of our country . . . are worth defending at all risks," he wrote. It would be a "disgrace" to allow our freedoms to be taken away "from us by violence, without a struggle, or be cheated out of them by tricks. . . ."

After the Boston Massacre, Adams and several other Bostonians came up with an idea for alerting others if—Adams would say "when"—the British government threatened the liberties of Bostonians again. They set up a Committee of Correspondence.

Correspondence means "an exchange of letters." If the British again took away any "rights of Englishmen," committee members would immediately send letters to other towns in the Massachusetts colony with the news.

This idea quickly spread to other colonies. Soon there was a great network of Committees of Correspondence. They would get news out quickly within each colony and also from one colony to another.

Of course these Patriot letter-writers didn't leave their quill pens and paper in their desk drawers while waiting for the next incident. They wrote to each other often, exchanging thoughts. Some of these thoughts would have been unthinkable just a few years earlier. Like independence. Little by little, that idea spread throughout the colonies.

Those who wanted independence were still in the minority. But who could say what would happen if the British government threatened their liberties once again?

Relations became strained between Great Britain and the colonies.

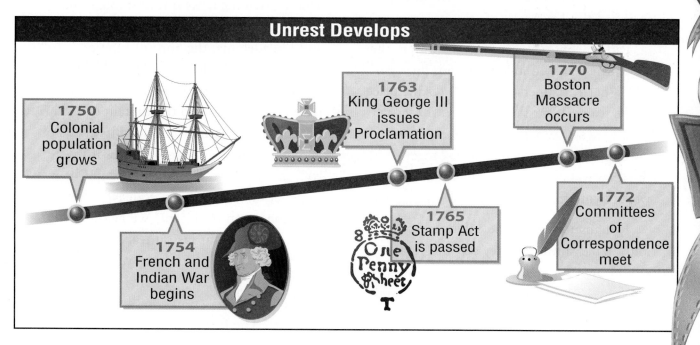

Unrest Develops

1750 Colonial population grows

1754 French and Indian War begins

1763 King George III issues Proclamation

1765 Stamp Act is passed

1770 Boston Massacre occurs

1772 Committees of Correspondence meet

One Penny Sheet

10 A Tea Party in Boston

Parliament Makes Another Mistake Did you ever hear the expression, "He was too clever for his own good"? It means that sometimes a person thinks he has a clever solution to a problem, when in fact all he does is make things worse.

You couldn't get a better description for what the British government did next. You'll remember that Parliament had left the tax on tea just to show the colonists that it had the right to tax them. And the colonists had left the boycott on tea just to show Parliament that it didn't.

Clearly, Parliament decided, that plan had not worked. British tea merchants had lost all their colonial customers. The Americans were buying tea smuggled in by Dutch merchants. And the government still hadn't collected more than a few pennies in taxes. So in 1773, Parliament came up with another plan. It passed the Tea Act.

Parliament's new plan was so "clever" that it's a little tricky to follow, but not impossible. What Parliament did was *lower* the price of the tea itself. At the same time *it kept the tax on the tea*. When you added the new, lower price of the tea and the tax together, the total was cheaper than the tea colonists were buying from the Dutch.

Parliament figured the colonists would know a bargain when they saw it. They would buy tea again from the British merchants. And when they did, they would be paying the tax to Great Britain! Soon 2,000 chests of tea were loaded aboard British ships bound for the American colonies. It was an idea that couldn't miss.

But it did. Parliament "was too clever for its own good." The Tea Act of 1773 just showed how poorly Parliament understood the colonists. This was a matter of principle for the colonists, not money. The principle was "no taxation without representation." They were not going to pay that tea tax, no matter what the price of British tea.

News Travels Fast

As British tea ships headed for the colonies, Committees of Correspondence swung into action. Soon the news spread through the colonies. In several ports, including New York and Philadelphia, the Sons of Liberty prevented the British ships from docking. In Philadelphia, for example, the Sons of Liberty sent a letter to the captain of a ship waiting in the harbor to unload its chests of tea. I wouldn't try to land that tea if I were you, said the letter. Your ship may just happen to be set on fire, and you yourself will be in for some rough treatment. We Pennsylvanians will never pay your tax on tea, for "no power on the face of the earth has a right to tax [us] without our consent." We are "passionately fond of freedom . . . and are determined to enjoy it." The British captain got the idea pretty quickly. He decided not to land.

No one was fooled by the Indian costumes worn by the colonists when they tossed the tea into Boston Harbor.

Similar happenings occurred in other colonial port cities. Some ship captains had their ships wait in the harbor, hoping for a change of heart. Others turned their ships around and headed home.

Not in Boston, however. Early in December three tea ships entered the harbor of that city. Citizens of the town gathered at a town meeting. They demanded that the governor of the colony order the ships to leave. The governor had no sympathy for Sam Adams and his bunch of trouble-makers. He refused.

At that point the colonists took matters into their own hands. On the night of December 16, 1773, a group of them dressed as Indians. They rowed out to the tea ships lying at anchor in the harbor and boarded them. They dumped every chest of tea aboard—342 of them—into the cold waters of the harbor. All of this was done in a quiet, businesslike fashion. When they were through, the "Indians" even swept the deck and put everything back in its proper place before leaving the ships. This was no secret operation. Many people in town knew it was going to happen. Carrying torches and lamps, they showed up at the shore to watch in silence as the chests of tea were thrown overboard. This event became known as the Boston Tea Party.

The Intolerable Acts

You can imagine the reaction of Parliament and the king when they got news of the Tea Party. They were outraged. That does it, they said. We are going to teach these colonists once and for all who makes the rules in this empire.

Parliament passed several laws to punish the people of Boston and the whole Massachusetts colony. One law closed the port of Boston until the colonists paid for the dumped tea. That meant no ships could go in and none could go out. For a city that depended on trade and fishing, this was a severe punishment. Parliament hoped that Boston's merchants and sea captains would be pressured into turning in the guilty persons or perhaps pay for the tea themselves. They did neither. Another law took away most of the Massachusetts colony's rights to self-government. The British also appointed an army general to be the governor of Massachusetts. They sent several thousand more troops to Boston—as if there weren't already more than enough. They ordered the colonists to put these troops up in their homes and even to feed them.

Making Enemies

Can you imagine how that must have felt to the colonists? Even a family that was loyal to Great Britain, even a family that opposed the actions of the Sons of Liberty, even a family that wanted to buy the British tea and pay the tea tax would feel humiliated and angry. The British government thought it was just punishing the colonies. In reality, it was losing friends and making enemies. Once again, Committees of Correspondence spread the news. American colonists everywhere were angry. These acts of Parliament were trampling on the "rights of Englishmen." Colonists called the new laws the Intolerable Acts because they could not tolerate or endure them. And they decided to stand together with the people of Boston to resist them.

This tax collector has been painted with melted tar and covered with feathers. He is also being forced to drink hot tea.

Help from the Other Colonies Parliament was right about one thing: the Intolerable Acts did make the people of Boston and the rest of Massachusetts suffer. But Parliament didn't figure on the other colonies coming to their aid.

Pennsylvania sent barrels of flour to the people of Massachusetts. New York sent them sheep. From South Carolina came sacks of rice; from Connecticut, money; from Virginia, corn and wheat.

Virginia's leaders went further. They set aside a day of fasting and prayer for the people of Boston. They also declared that the Intolerable Acts were a threat to liberty in all the colonies. If the king and Parliament could do these things to Massachusetts, what would stop them from doing the same to other colonies?

Then the Virginians took a bold step. They called for delegates from all the colonies to meet and discuss what to do next. This would be the second time delegates met to resist an act of Parliament. The first time was the Stamp Act Congress, and it had been successful. This time, though, the British government seemed determined not to back down.

The First Continental Congress

With Committees of Correspondence spreading the word, 56 colonial leaders assembled in Philadelphia in September 1774. They represented 12 of the 13 British colonies in North America. You can tell how important the colonists thought this meeting was by the

Who wasn't there? Only Georgia didn't send a delegation to the First Continental Congress.

people they chose to represent them. George Washington, Patrick Henry, and young Thomas Jefferson were there from Virginia. Sam Adams and his cousin John came from Massachusetts. New York sent John Jay, who later would serve on the Supreme Court of the United States. John Adams wrote in his diary, "There is in the Congress a collection of the greatest men upon this continent."

This meeting later became known as the First Continental Congress. The delegates talked together about their common problems. They expressed their anger at the British government. They issued a Declaration of Rights, saying that American colonists were entitled to all the "rights of Englishmen." They pointed out all the acts of Parliament since the French and Indian War that had been taking these rights away. They also told King George III that the colonists were still loyal to him and asked him to consider their complaints.

The members of the First Continental Congress did two more things. They voted to stop all trade with the British—buy nothing from them and sell nothing to them—until Parliament repealed the Intolerable Acts. And they agreed to meet again in May 1775 if

George Washington represented Virginia at the Continental Congress.

Parliament had still done nothing to restore their rights.

Talk about defiance! This was the most defiant act of the colonies yet. They had really thrown down a challenge to Great Britain.

But something else had happened, too—something that was hard to put your finger on. This "something" had no exact name. You couldn't put an exact date on when it started. But it was as important as any of the resolutions passed by the Continental Congress. Maybe those shipments of flour and rice and money to Boston from the other colonies were the start of it. Maybe it began with the Stamp Act Congress. Or maybe it had slowly been happening all along, before anyone was even aware of it. That "something" was that the colonies were coming together as never before.

Before this, each colony had thought of itself as separate from the others. Their inhabitants thought of themselves as Virginians or New Yorkers or Georgians. When they thought of an attachment to any other place, it was to Great Britain. Partly that was because each colony had more to do with the mother country than it did with the other colonies. And partly it was because colonists thought of themselves as British citizens, with all "the rights of Englishmen."

By the end of the First Continental Congress, many colonists were thinking of themselves as part of one country, rather than as people living in 13 different colonies. They were becoming more aware of the things they had in common. They were becoming more aware that they needed each other. Patrick Henry, that shrewd Virginian, captured this new mood perfectly. Speaking to the Continental Congress, he said, "The distinctions [differences] between Virginians, Pennsylvanians, New Yorkers, and New Englanders, are no more. I am not a Virginian but an American."

Maybes That Didn't Happen Maybe if King George III had been willing to pay attention to the colonists' pleas . . . maybe if Parliament had repealed the Intolerable Acts and promised to respect the colonists' "rights of Englishmen" . . .

maybe if the British government had taken all its troops out of the colonies . . . maybe if all those things had happened, or even some of them, war might still have been prevented.

Or maybe not. Maybe by that time the colonists had gone too far down the road toward independence to turn back. No one can say for sure what *might* have happened.

But we do know what *did* happen. We know that by the start of 1775, more and more colonists expected the quarrels with the mother country to end up in fighting. By spring, the militias in many colonies were preparing for war. The militia was made up of citizens who volunteered to be part-time soldiers.

In March, members of the Virginia state assembly debated whether their colony should prepare for war. Some opposed the idea. But Patrick Henry believed the time had come for action. Everyone present knew what a great speaker Henry was. As he rose to address the members, a hush fell over the room. Some of the earlier speakers had said that maybe Britain could still be persuaded to change its course. Here is Patrick Henry's answer:

> Shall we try argument? Sir, we have been trying that for the last ten years. . . . We must fight!

Virginians respond to Patrick Henry's "give me liberty or give me death!" speech.

Gentlemen may cry peace, peace—but there is no peace. The war is actually begun! The next gale that sweeps from the north will bring to our ears the clash of resounding arms! Our brethren are already in the field. Why stand we here idle? What is it the gentlemen wish? What would they have: Is life so dear, or peace so sweet, as to be purchased at the price of chains and slavery? Forbid it, almighty God!

And then Patrick Henry, standing tall, arms raised high, his voice clear as a bell, finished with the words that have stirred lovers of liberty ever since:

I know not what course others may take; but as for me, give me liberty, or give me death!

Patrick Henry was mistaken when he said that the war had actually begun. But three weeks after his stirring speech, the fighting did start. For several months, members of the militias throughout Massachusetts had been training to fight. These farmers and towns-people called themselves Minutemen, because, they said, they could be ready to fight on a minute's notice. To prepare for battle, the Minutemen had been collecting guns, gunpowder, and other supplies. They hid these supplies in the village of Concord, about 15 miles northwest of the city of Boston.

Do you remember that the British government had sent an army general to serve as the governor of Massachusetts? That new governor was General Thomas Gage. Somehow General Gage learned about those hidden supplies in Concord. He also learned that two Sons of Liberty who were the chief troublemakers in Boston, Sam Adams and John Hancock, were hiding out in the town of Lexington.

Lexington was on the way to Concord. General Gage figured he could kill two birds with one stone. He would send his troops to Lexington first and capture Adams and Hancock. The soldiers would then continue on to Concord and seize the Minutemen's hidden supplies.

General Gage's plan was to have his troops leave Boston in the dead of night. That way no one would notice, and they would take Lexington by surprise. Gage didn't know that the Sons of Liberty had gotten wind of his plan. Two Sons of Liberty, Paul Revere and William Dawes, got ready to ride ahead of the British soldiers and alert citizens along the way.

But there were two routes to Lexington. Which one would the redcoats take? One was longer, but it was entirely over land. The shorter route required that the troops first cross the Charles River by rowboat before starting the overland march.

The Minuteman is a symbol of Americans' willingness to defend their country.

Billy Dawes started out along the long route to Lexington. He galloped along in the dark of night, calling out to Patriot homes along the way that the redcoats were coming.

Paul Revere hung back, in case the British were taking the other route. He had already arranged for a signal to be sent to the waiting Sons of Liberty on the other shore. A young man would climb to the tower of the Old North Church in Boston and then signal with lanterns. He would hang one lantern in the tower if the British were taking the all-land route. If the troops were taking boats first to get to the shorter route, he would hang two. One if by land, two if by sea. When Paul Revere realized the British were planning to row across the river, he passed along the information to the signaler. That night, two lanterns burned brightly in the church tower. By sea! Now Paul Revere

and two friends hurried to a rowboat he had hidden. The three men rowed across the water ahead of the British troops. Once on shore, Revere borrowed a horse from one of the Sons of Liberty. Then he galloped off to carry the warning to Lexington and Concord. Stopping at every village and farm, he pounded on doors and sounded the alarm: "The redcoats are coming." In Lexington he was able to warn Sam Adams and John Hancock. The two men got away.

The Battle at Lexington

British troops arrived in Lexington at dawn, expecting to see no one. Imagine their surprise when they saw 70 Minutemen facing them on the village green. The leader of the Minutemen, Captain John Parker, told his men, "Stand your ground. Don't fire unless fired upon." Then he added, "But if they mean to have war, let it begin here."

Minutemen responded to the warning of the British plan and were waiting for the troops at Lexington.

E.B. Wollen/National Army Museum

There they stood—on the one side, 600 to 700 well-trained, well-armed men in handsome uniforms; on the other, a much smaller group in rough dress and with fewer weapons. The British officer ordered the Minutemen to leave.

Suddenly someone opened fire, and then both sides began shooting. Minutes later, eight Minutemen were dead, and another ten lay wounded.

The British caught both Billy Dawes and Paul Revere before they could get to Concord. However, another Patriot named Dr. Samuel Prescott rode off to Concord with the warning of a British attack.

The British troops next pushed on to Concord, where they destroyed some of the hidden supplies. Once again they were surprised to find Minutemen waiting for them. This time there were nearly 400 of them gathered at North Bridge, near the Concord village green.

Soldiers at the bridge opened fire. Minutemen fired back. After five minutes of fighting, the British decided to return to their base in Boston.

That long march back to Boston became a nightmare for the British soldiers. All those people who lived along the route had earlier been alerted by Paul Revere. They had seen the British as they marched toward Lexington in the early morning hours. Now they waited for their return—waited behind stone fences, behind barns, behind trees. When the soldiers, wearing their bright red uniforms, appeared, they were easy targets. All the way back to Boston, the shots rang out. Before the British troops got back to Boston that night, the Minutemen killed 73 of them and wounded another 200. That was nearly half the number who had started out. The colonists had losses too—nearly 50 men dead. Americans did not know it at the time, but the War for Independence had begun.

Concord Hymn

By the rude bridge that arched the flood,

Their flag to April's breeze unfurled,

Here once the embattled farmers stood,

And fired the shot heard round the world.

Many years later, Ralph Waldo Emerson wrote a poem to be read at a memorial ceremony celebrating the Battle of Concord. This is the first stanza.

May 10, 1775 Once again the leading men from every American colony gathered in Philadelphia for a Continental Congress. This time, though, was different. This time there had been fighting. This time men had died.

Most of the delegates to this Second Continental Congress weren't sure what to do next. They dreaded the thought of separating from Great Britain and their king. Couldn't Congress try again to patch up the quarrel with the mother country? At the same time, they could not ignore the fact that fighting had started. Shouldn't they take steps to prepare for more fighting, if it should come?

In the end the Second Continental Congress did both. Delegates wrote a **petition** to King George III. A petition is like a request. They told the king they were still loyal to him. There was no talk of independence. They said they didn't want to break up the British Empire. They only asked the king to make his government change its bad policies and restore their rights.

At the same time the Congress took steps to prepare for more fighting. John Adams of Massachusetts took the lead. Local militias are fine for fighting here and there, he

> **vocabulary**
> **petition** a formal written request signed by several people

This handbook, shown below, was printed in 1776 and describes how the militia should be trained. A farmer, right, prepares to join the other members of his local militia.

THE
MILITIA ACT;
TOGETHER WITH THE
RULES AND REGULATIONS
FOR THE
MILITIA.

Published by Order of the General Assembly.

BOSTON:
Printed by J. GILL, in Queen-Street.
M,DCC,LXXVI.

said. But we need to create a real American army—an "Army of the United Colonies."

At that moment, members of the Massachusetts militia were camped outside Boston, near the British troops. Those militiamen, said Adams, were ready to be the first soldiers in the new army.

And to lead it? How fortunate the Congress was, Adams continued, to have the right man for the job in that very room! He was a man of "great talents and excellent character." He was an experienced military leader from Virginia. As Adams continued to speak, all eyes turned to the tall man in military uniform standing in the back of the room. The man quickly turned and left the room. He wanted the delegates to be free to discuss him without his being present. The man was George Washington.

Adams was right. Washington was the perfect man to lead the Continental army, as it came to be called. He had gained his military experience in the French and Indian War. After that he returned to Mount Vernon, Virginia, to run his plantation. He was a member of the Virginia House of Burgesses and a supporter of the Patriot cause. And he was among the best-known men in the colonies. Everyone admired him for his devotion to duty, his cool head, and his strong will.

It was settled. Washington was to command the army. And the first members of that army would be the Massachusetts militiamen camped around Boston. They might be needed soon, for the news was that more soldiers were arriving from Great Britain.

Washington traveled to Massachusetts to take charge. Before he arrived, though, the militia fought an important battle near Boston.

There are two hills that overlook Boston. One was called Bunker Hill. The other Breed's Hill. Every general knows that it's a great advantage to control hills. From their tops you can fire down at the enemy below—especially if you have cannons. And the enemy has to fight its way uphill to defeat you. The British understood that, too, of course. But they were not very worried about those untrained Massachusetts militiamen nearby, and they did not bother to guard the hills. On the night of June 16, 1775,

On July 3, 1775, George Washington took command of the Continental army.

the militia suddenly marched to Breed's Hill and climbed it. All night they dug trenches, piling the earth into walls six feet high for their protection. When morning came, the British were surprised to see the colonial militia in control of the hill.

General Gage—remember him?—now worried that the militia would be able to fire on his troops below. They would even be able to use cannons to fire upon the British ships in the harbor. Gage decided he must drive the militia off the hill. What Gage didn't know was that the Massachusetts militia didn't even have cannons!

The next day, British soldiers marched up Breed's Hill. The colonists had only a small amount of ammunition. They couldn't afford to waste any.

They stood shoulder to shoulder behind the earthen walls they had built the night before. Their commander gave the order, "Don't fire until you see the whites of their eyes!" When the British got close, the militiamen opened fire. Hundreds of redcoats fell. The rest retreated down the hill.

Once more the British marched up the hill. Once more they were met with a hail of

Bunker Hill proved to be a very costly victory for the British.

bullets and driven back. But the colonists were now running out of ammunition. When the British marched up the hill a third time, the militia retreated.

The British won the hill but at a terrible cost. More than 1,000 soldiers were killed or wounded. Just as during that disastrous march back from Concord, the British lost about half their men. A British officer remarked that his army couldn't stand many more "victories" like this. The battle of Bunker Hill—that's what it was called, even though all the fighting took place on Breed's Hill— was very important to the colonists. They lost the hill, but they won new confidence. They were beginning to believe these citizen-soldiers could hold their own against one of the world's greatest armies—the British army.

Soon after, the colonists learned King George III's answer to their petition. Loyal to the king? Hah! Those colonists were nothing but traitors. Give back their "rights?" They have no rights except those I tell them they have. Withdraw my troops? I will show them. I will send 20,000 more men. I will crush them!

Coming to a Decision By the start of 1776, the argument with Great Britain had gone on for more than ten years. The fighting had gone on for almost one. And still, many colonists weren't sure they really wanted to strike out on the path of independence.

This gives you some idea about how difficult that decision was for many. A colony breaking away from a mother country—it had never been done before. Giving up a place in the world's greatest empire and all the advantages of being part of it—was that wise? Still, should the colonists do nothing to defend their rights and liberties? It was a very tough decision.

Tough, that is, until a 29-year-old-English immigrant wrote a pamphlet. After that the decision became very clear.

The immigrant's name was Thomas Paine, and he called his pamphlet *Common Sense*. Tom Paine had a great and rare skill. He could write about important ideas in the everyday language of the farmer, the worker, and the townsperson. If you could read at all, you could understand *Common Sense*. Probably half of all American colonists did read it. And after they did, they talked about it in their homes, on street corners, and in taverns and inns.

A lot of what Paine wrote was, just as he said, plain common sense. He got readers to think about his ideas not just by telling them what he thought but also by asking what *they* thought. Did it make any sense, Paine asked, for a huge continent like America to be ruled by a small island 3,000 miles away? Did it make sense for a people to be ruled by one man, just because he was born into a certain family? Wouldn't it be better to choose our rulers, rather than have one handed to us—someone who might be all wrong for the job but who got it only because his father had it before?

Americans should stop fooling themselves that monarchy—government headed by a king—would ever bring fair government to the people. It had never happened, and it never would. It was monarchy that was reducing the world to blood and ashes. Americans should abandon that form of government once and for all.

Thomas Paine's words rallied undecided colonists to the Patriot cause.

Independence National Historic Park

COMMON SENSE;
ADDRESSED TO THE
INHABITANTS
OF
AMERICA,
On the following interesting
SUBJECTS.
I. Of the Origin and Design of Government in general, with concise Remarks on the English Constitution.
II. Of Monarchy and Hereditary Succession.
III. Thoughts on the present State of American Affairs.
IV. Of the present Ability of America, with some miscellaneous Reflections.

Man knows no Master save creating HEAVEN,
Or those whom choice and common good ordain.
THOMSON.

PHILADELPHIA;
Printed, and sold, by R. BELL, in Third-Street.
MDCCLXXVI.

IN CONGRESS, JULY 4, 1776.

The unanimous Declaration of the thirteen united States of America.

It was an act of courage to sign the Declaration of Independence.

Paine said that it was just common sense for Americans to cut off all ties to Great Britain, to be independent and create a government of their own. Americans didn't need a king, he said. They could live in a land where "the law is king," not some person wearing a crown in a faraway land. The more they thought about it, the more Americans agreed. They didn't need the British Parliament and king to rule them. They had plenty of experience in choosing their own leaders and ruling themselves. Perhaps it really was time, then, to separate and go their own way.

The Declaration of Independence

In June 1776, the Second Continental Congress took up the question of independence. They agreed that the time had come to separate from Great Britain. The Congress chose a committee to write a declaration, or statement. The purpose of such a declaration was to explain to the world why the colonies were breaking away from Great Britain.

The committee chosen to write the declaration included John Adams, Benjamin Franklin, and a young, tall, redheaded Virginian, Thomas Jefferson. Which one should do the main writing? Benjamin Franklin and George Washington were probably two most famous Americans alive. John Adams was one of the first leaders to speak out in favor of independence. But Thomas Jefferson already had a reputation as a fine writer and was chosen by Franklin and Adams to write the document.

What Jefferson produced became the most famous document in American history, and one of the most famous in the history of the entire world. Of course Jefferson wanted the world to know all the bad things this king had done, all the rights he had taken away. So he listed each of them.

But Jefferson did more, much more. He explained why these acts of the king made it right for the colonists to break with Britain.

We hold these truths to be self-evident, that all men are created equal, that they are endowed by their Creator with certain unalienable rights, that among these are life, liberty, and the pursuit of happiness.

Jefferson continued by stating, "That to secure these rights, governments are instituted [created] . . ." In other words, the reason we have governments is to protect our rights.

What if a government doesn't protect those rights but actually takes them away? Then, said Jefferson, people have the right to create new governments for themselves. That's what the people of the 13 colonies were now doing.

On July 4, 1776, Congress adopted this Declaration of Independence. On that day the American colonies became independent states. Together, they made up the United States of America.

During the next month, in towns and cities across the land, crowds gathered to hear

Colonists celebrated the signing of the Declaration of Independence by raising Liberty Poles.

the Declaration of Independence read aloud. Everywhere in the new United States of America, church bells rang out. Soldiers fired cannons and shot off guns. Citizens lit great bonfires in celebration.

Meanwhile back in Philadelphia the mood among some of the delegates to the Second Continental Congress was a little more serious. The 56 men who signed the Declaration knew that if the revolution failed, the king would probably put them to death. Benjamin Franklin summed up the need for all the new states to work together. "Gentlemen," he said, "we must all hang together, [or] else we shall all hang separately."

atriot Problems During the first part of the war, "hanging separately" seemed like a real possibility. When you look at some of the problems the Americans faced, you can see that their chances of winning were not that great.

For one thing, the 13 new states may have been united, but their people certainly were not. Many remained loyal to the king and to Great Britain. These people were called Loyalists. Many of them moved to Great Britain or Canada, but others stayed in America and helped the British. About 50,000 Loyalists actually fought in the war on the side of Great Britain.

For another thing, Great Britain had one of the largest armies in the world. And that was even before you added the 50,000 Loyalists. On top of that the British hired about 30,000 professional soldiers from other countries. Soldiers for hire are called mercenaries. Counting the mercenaries, Great Britain's army was five times larger than the American army. The British could also count on their Indian allies in the West.

The British soldiers were well-trained fighters. Commanders could count on having their soldiers for a certain number of years and had time to train them for battle.

General Washington would have loved an arrangement like that. You'll remember that he had to build an army from scratch. His army was made up mainly of farmers—amateurs, not professional soldiers.

Also, Washington never knew how many soldiers he could count on at any one time. Some joined the Continental army for a three-year term. Most volunteered to serve for less than a year. And some signed up for only three months. Some would join the Continental army when the fighting got near their village or farm. Then they would leave it once the British troops moved on. Soldiers would often return to their farms at planting time and harvesting time. Lots of men did serve at one time or another, it is true. But with all these comings and goings, can you imagine how difficult it was to train an army?

Posters like this one were used to find soldiers for the Continental army.

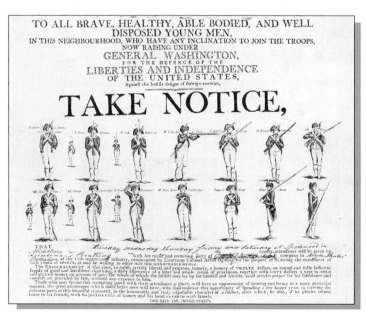

Then, too, Great Britain was the wealthiest nation in the world. The British could supply their army with whatever it needed. The American army, though, was often short of cannons, gunpowder, food, and other supplies, including uniforms. All through the war, most American soldiers fought in their own clothes. Several times during the war, General Washington had to write Congress that if it didn't come up with money for supplies and pay soon, "the army must absolutely break up."

As for a navy, the British had the greatest in the world. They had 100 times as many warships as the Americans had.

Certainly none of that looked very good for the Americans.

Americans had a few things going for them, though. For one, they were fighting on their own land. Can you see why that was important? It meant that fresh troops and supplies were often available nearby, while the British had to ship everything—including troops—from 3,000 miles away. Also, it makes a difference when one side is fighting to defend its own homes, its families, and its freedom while the other side is just fighting for pay.

Another advantage the American side had was the huge size of the country. Even if the British won in one part of the country, American armies could always retreat to another, where the British could not get them. Tom Paine wrote that the American plan would be like a game of checkers: "We can move out of *one* square to let you come in," he said to the British, "in order that we may afterwards take two or three for one." Since we can keep moving around, he said, "we can always prevent a total defeat."

Support from Women and Black Americans

The Patriot side could also count on important support from women. Women worked in army camps. They washed, cooked, nursed the wounded, and made gunpowder. There were even times when women went onto the battlefields, though they weren't supposed to. In one battle fought under a blazing sun, Mary Ludwig Hays brought her husband's cannon crew water from a nearby stream. She carried so many pitchers of water to the thirsty men that they came to call her Molly Pitcher.

According to legend, Molly's husband became ill during the battle. The other members of his cannon crew had been killed. Molly loaded and fired the cannon by herself

According to legend, Molly Pitcher helped the Patriots at the Battle of Monmouth.

until other soldiers arrived to take over. We don't know if that story is true, but it is certainly true that many American farm women knew how to handle a gun.

One of them was Deborah Sampson. Sampson dressed in men's clothing and joined the army. It was only when she became ill that doctors found out she was a woman. A number of other women served as messengers and spies.

But of course women didn't have to be on a battlefield to help the Patriot cause. They made their greatest contribution at home. In addition to doing the work they had always done, they also did the work of the men who had gone to fight. There were many women who kept the family farm going or the family business running.

About 5,000 blacks fought on the American side in the Revolutionary War. Most of them were free men from the northern states. They took part in almost every battle, starting with the very first at Bunker Hill. There were several black regiments from New England states.

But black Americans were divided over the Revolution, just as white Americans were. In fact, some southern states were even opposed to blacks joining the Continental army. They were always worrying about slave uprisings, and they did not like the idea of black people having guns—even blacks ready to fight for American independence!

In addition, black people knew that even if the United States succeeded in winning independence, that would not end slavery. It is hard to be enthusiastic about fighting for a country that wants to keep people like you in slavery.

The British knew that very well. Soon after fighting started, they offered freedom to any slave who would fight on Great Britain's side. Several thousand slaves risked their lives in running away so they could accept the offer. As fighting during the war reached slaveholding areas of the country, many slaves fled to the protection of the British. The British navy, in fact, carried several thousand of these escaped slaves to Canada, where they started free settlements.

An officer of the Continental army, shown on the right, meets a group of black soldiers from the Rhode Island regiment.

An Early British Victory Things went badly for the Americans during the early part of the war. Hardly three months after Americans lit bonfires to celebrate the Declaration of Independence, a large British army assembled in New York City to do battle with Washington's still untrained army.

The British defeated the Americans easily and almost trapped them. That might have ended the war then and there. Led by Washington, however, the Americans escaped from the city.

It was during that battle for New York City that a 24-year-old Connecticut schoolteacher named Nathan Hale won fame with words that inspired the Patriots. Hale was caught serving as a spy for the Americans and was hanged by the British. His last words have been quoted by patriotic people for more than 200 years: "I only regret that I have but one life to lose for my country."

After their narrow escape from New York, the Americans retreated all the way across New Jersey and into Pennsylvania, with the British close behind. Luckily, it was getting late in the year. Winter was a hard time to fight battles. The British were satisfied to take control of New York and New Jersey, and stop for the winter. There would be time enough in the spring to finish off the Americans. It was at this moment that Washington's leadership began to pay off for the Americans. Other generals might have panicked after facing such a setback. Not Washington. Whether he won a battle or lost, he remained the same steady person. Soldiers admired him, and they were willing to follow him into battle.

Battle, however, was not what Washington wanted. He knew his untrained troops were no match for the experienced British army in big head-on battles. Washington's plan for winning the war required patience. It can be summed up this way: Keep the Continental army moving—there was Tom Paine's checkerboard. Stop and fight the British now and then, but don't get into a major battle. Use the time to build up the army and train it.

The British burned New York City behind the retreating Continental army.

This plan meant the American army would not win many battles. But they wouldn't lose many, either. Meanwhile, as the war went on, the British people might tire of paying for it. Then a few big American victories, and who knows? They might stop supporting the war.

This famous painting by Emmanuel Leutze of Washington crossing the Delaware River was painted many years after the event.

A Surprise Attack

Washington realized that the American people could tire of the war, too. So could his army, if it kept suffering defeats. Washington needed a quick victory or two to raise the spirits of his soldiers and also of the nation.

He therefore planned a surprise attack on British mercenaries—remember the mercenaries, the troops the British hired from other countries? These mercenaries came from the German state of Hesse, so they were called Hessians. The Hessians were camped in Trenton, New Jersey, just across the Delaware River from Washington's troops in Pennsylvania. Washington knew that no one would expect him to move his troops across the ice-filled Delaware River.

That's exactly why he did it. On Christmas night, 1776, shivering American soldiers stepped into the long rowboats that would carry them across the river. By four o'clock in the morning, all 2,400 of Washington's men were on the New Jersey side of the river.

The Continentals marched the nine miles to Trenton in the dark of night. Then, as day broke, they attacked the sleeping Hessians. What a surprise! What confusion! After a short fight, 900 Hessians surrendered. The Continental army captured not only the enemy soldiers but also their weapons and supplies.

Eight days later, Washington won another victory. Again, he surprised British soldiers and defeated them, this time at Princeton, New Jersey. Just as Washington hoped, the victories at Trenton and Princeton raised the spirits of Americans and especially of the army.

ritain's Master Plan Those spirits wouldn't stay high for very long, if the British could help it. In fact, British generals had a plan to knock the Americans right out of the war before the year was over.

This was the plan. The Hudson River runs north and south in New York State. The British aimed to win control of the entire Hudson River valley. That would cut off New England from the other states, dividing the Americans in two. The British would then be able to defeat the rebels one part at a time— first New England, then the rest.

That summer, General John Burgoyne (bur *GOYN*) led a large British army southward from Canada into New York State. The plan was for the main British army in New York City to start moving north soon after Burgoyne entered New York State. At about the same time, a third, smaller British force in western New York State would move east. The three British armies would meet near Albany, on the Hudson River. At that point, it would be all over for the upstart Americans. Only it didn't happen. General William Howe was in charge of the main British army in New York. Howe wanted to capture Philadelphia first before starting north along the Hudson. Philadelphia was America's largest city. It was the meeting place of the Continental Congress. What a blow to American spirits if the British were to take it!

That was General Howe's thinking, anyway. Howe was sure he could capture Philadelphia and still have time to send his armies north to meet Burgoyne. He was

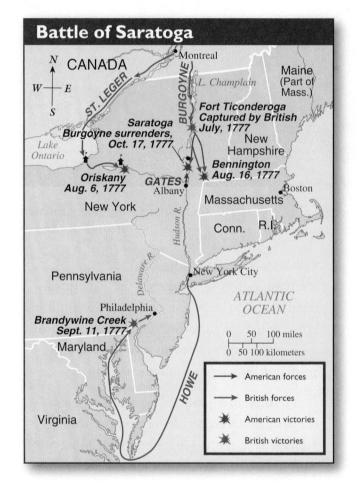

The British plan didn't work because only one British force arrived at Saratoga.

wrong. By the time he captured Philadelphia, there was no time left to get his troops back to New York. Howe didn't even try.

Meanwhile, the third British force—the one moving eastward across New York State— under the command of Barry St. Leger ran into American soldiers along the way. Those British soldiers never made it to Albany either.

So there was Burgoyne, moving south in New York State, suddenly finding his army all alone. The only ones there to meet him were American soldiers under General Gates—thousands and thousands of them. In October 1777, the British and Americans fought at Saratoga, north of Albany. The Americans won, and 6,000 of Great Britain's best soldiers surrendered.

The victory at Saratoga was a great turning point in the war. Not just because it was a great victory but also because it brought us a new ally—France. Do you remember how the French and the English had been fighting for a hundred years? And how the French lost all their North American colonies to Great Britain in the French and Indian War? Well, ever since, they had been burning for revenge.

New Allies

One way for France to get revenge on Great Britain was to help the American colonies break away. Soon after the colonies declared independence, France secretly started sending them money and supplies. If they did it openly, Great Britain would probably declare war on France, and the French king did not want that.

The Americans hoped for more. They wanted France to jump into the war with both feet. Every time they asked the French, though, they got the same answer: Show us first that you have a real chance of defeating the British, and then we might consider joining forces with you. The victory at Saratoga showed France that America could win. Several months after Saratoga, the French did come into the war on the side of the Americans. France sent money, equipment, and soldiers. Most important, as you will soon see, France also sent a large naval fleet to help the Americans. It's quite possible that without the French, the Americans would not have won.

Later, Spain and the Netherlands, two more old enemies of Great Britain, entered the war on the American side. These changes meant that Great Britain would have to fight not only in North America but also in Europe and other parts of the world. All because three British armies failed to meet as planned in Albany.

It was a great moment when General Gates accepted General Burgoyne's surrender after the Battle of Saratoga.

18 Valley Forge

Hard Winter Now came the worst time of the war for the Continental army. It was the winter of 1777–1778. The British had taken Philadelphia.

Twice, General Washington had sent his troops into battle near Philadelphia. Twice the British had defeated them. With cold weather coming on, Washington had to choose a place to camp for the winter. The place he chose was called Valley Forge, an open field about 20 miles from Philadelphia.

Snow was already on the ground when the troops arrived in Valley Forge. They put up their tents and began building huts with whatever wood they could find. Before long they had built 2,000 of them—drafty, dirty, and cold, but at least providing a roof over the heads of the men. Each had a fireplace but no windows. The smoke from the fires made men cough as if their lungs would burst.

The winter at Valley Forge could have broken the spirit of the Continental army.

That winter was a terrible one. Supplies did not arrive. Blankets were scarce. There was not food enough to go around. With no boots or shoes, the men wrapped their feet in rags. General Washington later said, "You might have tracked the army to Valley Forge by the blood of their feet." An officer from Connecticut tells us how bad things were in his diary:

> It snows. I'm sick. Eat nothing. No whiskey. No forage. Lord, Lord, Lord . . . cold and uncomfortable. I am sick, discontented, and out of humor. Poor food. Hard lodging. Cold weather. Fatigue. Nasty clothes. Nasty cookery. Vomit half my time. Smoked out of my senses. The Devil's in it. I can't endure it. Why are we sent here to starve and freeze? . . . I have

Courtesy of, The Valley Forge Historical Society

Many Europeans came to support the Patriot cause, including (from left to right) Steuben, Pulaski, Kosciusko, and Lafayette.

left at home a charming wife, pretty children, good beds, good food, good cookery. . . . Here all confusion, smoke and cold, hunger and filthiness. A pox on my bad luck.

At least 2,500 soldiers died of disease or exposure at Valley Forge that winter. That means that every single day, soldiers had to bury 25 or 30 of their comrades. Some men deserted, which means they simply sneaked out of camp and went home. At the start of winter, Washington's army numbered about 7,000 men. At the end of winter, there were only about 4,000 left.

The winter at Valley Forge was a time of testing for the men of the Continental army. They passed the test. Much of the credit has to go to their commander, George Washington.

A Man of Character

Character. What did people mean when they said that George Washington was a man of great character? They meant he was honest. They meant that he cared for his men, and that he was fair with them. They meant that you always knew where Washington stood and that he kept his word. They meant that he respected others and that you could depend on him. They meant that Washington was the kind of man you would always want on your side.

Washington also knew enough to put able men in charge of important tasks. For example,

in February, when things were at their worst, a balding, red-faced man appeared at Washington's headquarters to offer his services. His name was Baron Frederick von Steuben (STOO bun). Washington could tell that this fellow knew how to train men to be soldiers, and that was what Washington needed. He hired von Steuben. The German officer taught the men about soldiering, and he drilled them over and over. By spring, General Washington had a well-trained army for the very first time.

Von Steuben was only one of a number of Europeans who were inspired to help the American cause. Another was a 19-year-old Frenchman named the Marquis de Lafayette. As soon as he heard that fighting had begun in America, Lafayette decided to join the Americans in their fight for liberty. "I am persuaded," he said, "that the human race was created to be free, and that I am born to serve that cause." Washington took a great liking to this daring Frenchman, and Lafayette quickly became one of his most trusted aides.

Others arrived as well to help the American cause. From Poland came Thaddeus Kosciusko and Casimir Pulaski. Pulaski was wounded in battle and died, while Kosciusko later returned to Poland to fight for liberty there. Many others were inspired to fight for American liberty.

Another Plan Meanwhile, the British generals came up with another plan to win the war. For three years, said the generals, we've been fighting the Americans in the North. We've won most of the battles, so we're not losing the war. But we're not winning it either.

To win, we have to beat down the rebellion. That means we have to really defeat the Continental army. Every time we have a chance to do that, though, General Washington and his army slip away from us. The British generals thought: Suppose we shift the battle to the South? That would give us several big advantages. For one thing, most of the Continental army is in the North. We will catch them off guard. Also, there are lots of Loyalists in the South. We can count on them to help us with food and supplies. After we take the South, we'll have the Continental army squeezed between our forces there and our other armies in the North.

The plan turned out to be pretty successful for a while. The British navy brought soldiers from their base in New York to Savannah, Georgia. The soldiers quickly captured that city. Within a year they controlled the whole state of Georgia. Soon after, the British took Charleston, South Carolina, and handed the Americans their worst defeat of the war. From there, British troops successfully went on to control a large part of the South.

However, the British were still not able to crush the enemy. American military commanders in the South followed the George Washington strategy. Small battles, yes. Big battles, no. Never risk the whole army in one big fight. Also, southerners knew their land

better than the British did. They set up secret bases in the swamps of South Carolina. They would come out of the swamps to attack small groups of British soldiers. Then, as suddenly as they had appeared, they were gone.

This kind of hit-and-run fighting is called **guerrilla** warfare. A general named Francis Marion was so successful at it that he came to be called the Swamp Fox. So the British armies won many small battles, but they could never catch up to the American troops to defeat them in a big one. And in time, the American troops began to win their share of the battles.

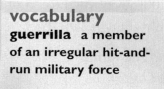

vocabulary
guerrilla a member of an irregular hit-and-run military force

War in the West

Meanwhile, in the West, a young Virginian named George Rogers Clark attacked several British forts near the Great Lakes. The British were using these forts to stir up their Indian allies to attack American settlers.

On July 4, 1778, Clark and a company of 175 Virginia militiamen captured the first of these forts without firing a shot. Later, Clark captured two more. His victories drove the British out of part of the land between the Appalachian Mountains and the Mississippi River.

*The sea battle between the **Bonhomme Richard** and the **Serapis** took over four hours.*

A Victory at Sea

The tiny American navy, of course, was no match for the great British fleet. But American warships put up a good fight when they met one British ship at a time. John Paul Jones was the commander of the American ship *Bonhomme* (BAHN um) *Richard* when it came upon the British warship *Serapis* off the coast of Great Britain. The two ships opened fire. Soon the deck of the American ship was in flames. The British commander then demanded that Jones surrender. Jones replied, "I have not yet begun to fight!"

And fight he did. His own ship, the *Bonhomme Richard,* sank, but not before Jones and his men climbed aboard the *Serapis* and took it over. This was one of the most famous naval battles in our country's history.

Benedict Arnold

During this time, George Washington suffered one of his greatest disappointments. It was not a defeat on the battlefield. It was a defeat of the spirit. One of his bravest and finest generals, and one of Washington's favorites, went over to the enemy.

His name was Benedict Arnold. He had helped win the battle of Saratoga. He had been promoted to general and his future in the American army was bright. In 1780, General Washington placed Benedict Arnold in command of West Point, a fort on the Hudson River.

But Benedict Arnold still did not feel appreciated enough. And he liked to spend much more money than he could afford on luxuries. So in exchange for a large sum of money, Arnold agreed to turn over West Point to the British.

The plot was discovered in time, but Arnold himself escaped and joined the British forces. Americans were shocked to learn of Benedict Arnold's treason. Even today, the name "Benedict Arnold" is a synonym for a traitor.

British Mistake Now came the big mistake that cost Great Britain the war. The general in charge of British armies in the South was Lord Charles Cornwallis. Cornwallis had spent a year chasing American troops in the South.

He finally decided to move his army to Virginia. Cornwallis believed that if he could defeat the American soldiers in Virginia, he would crush the rebellion.

In the summer of 1781, Cornwallis chose a small Virginia town called Yorktown for his base. Yorktown is located on the York River, which flows into the sea. Cornwallis chose this place so that the British navy could reach him easily with troops and supplies.

Normally, it's not a good idea to set up a base with a river at your back. If you have to retreat, you have no place to go. But Lord Cornwallis felt safe there. He had one third of all the British soldiers in America with him. And he could count on the British navy to bring him even more, if he needed them.

Washington Responds

At the very moment that Cornwallis was setting up his base at Yorktown, George Washington was meeting with a French general in Rhode Island. The French, you see, had sent an army to help the Americans. There was also a large French fleet on its way to help out.

Washington and the French general Rochambeau (row sham BOW) were making a plan to attack the British armies in New York City when the news about Yorktown arrived.

Washington immediately saw Cornwallis's mistake. Forget about attacking New York, he said. The American and French armies should hurry to Virginia. Together, they had enough men to trap Cornwallis with his army's back against the river. If the French fleet could get there in time, it could keep the British navy from helping Cornwallis. Then Cornwallis would have to surrender. In one single victory, Washington might end the war! Yorktown was 500 miles away. George

Yorktown was on a peninsula that the Americans and the French surrounded on land and on sea.

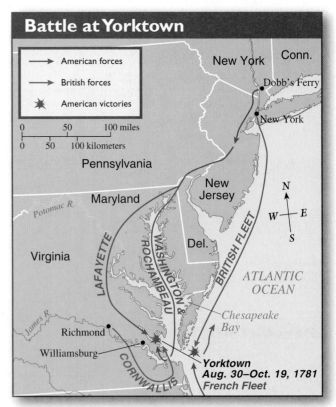

Battle at Yorktown

American forces
British forces
American victories

0   50   100 miles
0   50   100 kilometers

New York   Conn.
Dobb's Ferry
New York
Pennsylvania
New Jersey
N
Potomac R.   Maryland
W — E
Del.
S
LAFAYETTE
WASHINGTON & ROCHAMBEAU
BRITISH FLEET
Virginia
ATLANTIC OCEAN
Chesapeake Bay
James R.
Richmond
Williamsburg
CORNWALLIS
Yorktown
Aug. 30–Oct. 19, 1781
French Fleet

The American Revolution ended soon after the surrender at Yorktown.

Washington had started his military career with a 500-mile journey. That one ended in disappointment. Now he was to set out on another one, with the chance of winning the victory of a lifetime.

It took more than a month for the armies to get to Yorktown. Then it took a few more days to dig a great half-ring of trenches around the town, surrounding it by land. On October 9, at five o'clock in the afternoon, the first cannon was fired, and the battle had begun. For once, it was General Washington who had the most guns and cannons. For once, it was General Washington who had the most men.

Cornwallis looked out to the sea for help, but none ever came. The French fleet had driven off the British fleet. Cornwallis's army was on its own.

Each day, Washington moved his army closer and closer, tightening the half-ring a little more. Washington rode back and forth among his men, taking his chances like everyone else that a bullet might strike him. The troops cheered and pressed on.

Cornwallis was trapped. For several more days, cannons roared. Finally the British general saw that it was useless to continue. On October 17, Cornwallis surrendered.

Two days later the American and French armies formed two long lines. The defeated British troops marched between them and left the town. As they did, a British army band played a tune that all of them knew. It was a tune that went with a nursery rhyme. A strange tune to play at a time like this, you might think. But the words, which every British soldier knew, were the reason it was chosen:

If buttercups buzzed after the bee,
If boats were on land, churches on sea,
If ponies rode men, and if grass ate the
    corn
And cats should be chased into holes by
    the mouse,
If the mammas sold babies for half a
    crown,
If summer were spring, and the other way
    'round,
Then all the world would be
    upside down.

A ragtag collection of citizen soldiers had defeated one of the world's greatest armies. A group of colonies had succeeded in gaining independence from a mother country for the first time ever. The United States of America had been created, and a great British Empire had been humbled. In the peace treaty that followed, Britain agreed that the colonies were now "free and independent states."

A Final Word

The American Revolution produced many heroes. Some became famous: George Washington, John Paul Jones, Francis Marion.

Most of the heroes, though, were ordinary people. Their names are never written in the history books. They were the Minutemen on Lexington Green. They were the soldiers who shivered at Valley Forge. They were the men who dashed out of their swamp hideouts to strike at the British army.

They were also the women who brought food and water to the men in battle, took care of the wounded and the sick, and kept farms and shops running. They were the farm families who shared their food with the soldiers and the townspeople who gave the soldiers housing. They were the women, children, and old men who made weapons and gunpowder for them. They were the boys and girls who helped produce the food and the clothing that the American soldiers needed.

When the war was over, people everywhere asked, "How could the American colonies have won a war against one of the great military powers in the world?" The answer to this question was really not difficult to find. The main reason the Revolutionary War was won is that ordinary Americans refused to lose it.

There were many steps that led to independence.

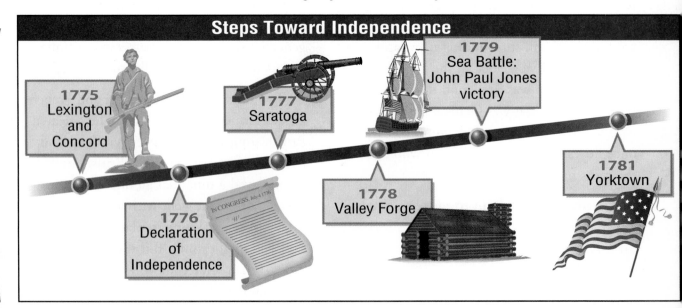

Steps Toward Independence

1775
Lexington
and
Concord

1776
Declaration
of
Independence

1777
Saratoga

1778
Valley Forge

1779
Sea Battle:
John Paul Jones
victory

1781
Yorktown

ally a nation that has promised to help another nation in wartime

assembly a group of representatives who gather to make laws

boycott an organized campaign in which people refuse to have any dealings with a particular group or country in order to force a change of policy

frontier the newly settled area on the edge of the unsettled area or wilderness

guerrilla a member of an irregular hit-and-run military force

immigrant a person from one country who comes into another country to live there

militia a body of armed citizens prepared for military service at any time

petition a formal written request signed by several people

repeal to cancel or do away with